Summary of

Waypoints:

My Scottish Journey

Barbara Robert

Table of Contents

Chapter 1

"It was so secretive that no one at any point affirmed that I was being considered for the fundamental job, however, I knew. It took my breath away to figure I could try and be on the edge for such a notable figure," He composes. "I needed to remind myself to unwind and allow them to see how I could manage the person."

However the job eventually went to Daniel Craig — "the criticism I got reduced to the way that I wasn't restless enough ordinarily," Heughan uncovers — the entertainer doesn't seem to hold onto any bad sentiments. "It was very much an encounter," He told EW. "It was a phase in my life where I likely wasn't prepared for it, yet I can't help thinking about what might have occurred if I had got it.

Since Craig has as of late completed his run and the renowned spy, and the job may by and by being available to all, could Heughan think about a subsequent endeavor? "See, each English entertainer surely has been discussed for the job. I wouldn't want anything more than to see a Scottish Bond," he said. "Perhaps I'm too old at this point. I realize that they've been looking at making him more youthful. I feel like that is where they will go, however, who can say for sure what's in their psyche."

Alongside his experience trying out for the job of Bond, Heughan additionally opens up in the book about his young life, his relationship with his dad, and his initial encounters as an entertainer, including how he felt double-crossed by Stranger's imaginative group over the portrayal of Jamie's attack in the show's most memorable season.

He talked about his part in "Foreigner" in his diary, "Waypoints: My Scottish Process."

In the show's most memorable season, he recorded a scene that incorporated a "pointless" shot of his penis.

Notice

He has said that he felt sold out by the imaginative group behind "Stranger" after recording an assault scene in which a "pointless" shot of his penis was incorporated.

He has been assuming the part of Jamie Fraser, an eighteenth-century High country fighter in the Starz series, starting around 2014.

While the show as of late broadcasted its 6th season, the Scottish entertainer conceded that a scene back in season one, in which his personality is physically attacked by his foe Dark Jack Randall (Tobias Menzies), pushed the limits of what he was OK with.

Writing in his diary "Waypoints: My Scottish Process," He reviewed that from the beginning of the show's shooting, he knew that the series — which depends on a progression of smash hit books by American writer Diana Gabaldon — was driving his personality to a "dim, depressing and testing place."

Taking note that he was authoritatively expected to film bare scenes and that the show has "never got some distance from sexual viciousness," Heughan composed that he emphatically felt it wasn't essential for him to strip down for the merciless assault scene, which finished up the show's most memorable season.

Chapter 2

"This wasn't a second where I felt that being bare would add to the repulsiveness of what Jamie goes through in that palace prison as a type of discipline, enslavement, and embarrassment," He composed.

"I pushed back, thinking that nakedness sexualized a terrible encounter for my personality, and it started truly a discussion," he proceeded. "Imaginative discussions are an element, everything being equal, great workmanship is made by scrutinizing reality and we as a whole need to hit the nail on the head."

At last, He and the imaginative group came to an understanding that Jamie would just be seen as exposed to the repercussions of the assault. It was concluded in post production that the unequivocal shots would be left "on the cutting room floor" and not displayed to crowds.

He proceeded to compose that assuming the scene was to be shot today, "it would have been taken care of in an unexpected way," adding: "Circumstances are different. The chicken shot was superfluous and double-crossed my confidence in the imaginative group a little. We don't have to see the frightfulness to envision what the characters go through. A creative mind is much more impressive."

His comments reverberate remarks he made to Insider in mid-2022 in front of the arrival of the show's 6th season.

Thinking about a similar scene, he told diversion correspondent Libby Torres: "I didn't feel that upheld, glancing back at it looking back."

He uncovered why the James Bond projecting group gave him the boot from a tryout.

As revealed by Amusement Week after week, He partook in his impending diary Waypoints: My Scottish Process about his disheartening experience in the wake of trying out to depict the exemplary English covert operative. "At the point when I took on the job I had gone somewhere else, notwithstanding, the criticism I got reduced to the way that I wasn't restless enough commonly," He composed. "I'm dependably quick to take on analysis so I can work on as an entertainer, however, the idea appeared to be that I was missing the mark on quality in my genuine personality. I was unable to see what bearing that would have on assuming the part, however, it was none of my concern, and intended to be."

While He purportedly came up with the short tense they were looking for, he owned up to his past absence of fearlessness. "It was anything but an issue of turning into a terrible kid. I understood that the edge the Bond group looked for could be accomplished through fearlessness, which to be fair I was positively missing at that point." Assuming the Bond makers had acknowledged Him, he would have been the second Scottish entertainer ahead of the pack, second just to the late Sean Connery.

Notwithstanding the 42-year-old entertainer's past deficiencies, the opposition was seemingly savage to play James Security. Be that as it may, the entertainer, who has since accomplished approval on Foreigner, addresses where the establishment might pursue Daniel Craig's run finished with No Opportunity to Pass on. "I realize that they've been looking at making him more youthful. I feel like that is where they will go, yet who can say for sure what's in their psyche," Heughan expressed.

Regardless of whether He has the opportunity to play the immortal English Mystery Administration specialist, he featured as an Exceptional Air Administration administrator in the 2021 film SAS: Red Notification. He reviewed how time on the activity thrill ride was a "praise to the Bond world. "We worked intimately with Andy McNab, who is an exceptionally brightened English Unique Powers administrator," he said. "It's founded on him, the person, so as it were, it's a more intriguing job than Bond."

Notwithstanding his bombed 007 tryouts, Heughan likewise reported on Foreigner's impending seventh season. He uncovered that the creation is "part of the way through" the recording system of the 16-episode season. In any case, that show won't be the main true-to-life variation of book writer Diana Gabaldon's universe since Starz reported Foreigner: Blood of My Blood, a prequel series following Jamie Fraser's folks, Ellen MacKenzie and Brian Fraser.

Chapter 3

His personality on "Stranger," Jamie Fraiser, is known for the conflict he's persevered on screen. However he endures floggings and wrecks, Jamie Fraiser is pushed by an enthusiastic relationship with another person, Claire Randall.

He subtleties the legendary story of his life off-screen in a recently delivered diary named "Waypoints: My Scottish

Process." In the book, Heughan ponders his excursion to turning into an effective entertainer while climbing Scotland's West Good Country Way.

"This isn't Jamie Fraser, the ruler of men. This is an entertainer who believes he's assuming the part of a hillwalker," he says. "Yet, I battled. I nearly surrendered. I wound up lost in favor of Loch Lomond in obscurity. Furthermore, it was only after I truly kind of dialed back and partook in the excursion that I started to see the value in the actual path."

His process drove him to establish a non-benefit association called My Pinnacle Challenge to motivate others to carry on with a sound, dynamic life. The more than $6 million raised so far has helped various causes from hunger alleviation to disease research.

On setting out on his climbing process

"I prepared out and was to set off into the wilds. Some lady came dependent upon me and she remembered me from the Program, and it was truly a truly pleasant trade. It's fascinating because I set off on this single excursion. I needed to carve out an opportunity to reflect and the minutes where I met individuals made the excursion way seriously fulfilling."

On recounting 'Romeo and Juliet' to himself on the trip

"It's fascinating because, I think, I hadn't at any point truly reviewed it. What's more, someplace in the obscurity of my psyche, it emerged alongside all the other things that were most likely discharged there. I ended up dropping into craziness: conversing with myself, conversing with the nearby fauna, the mushrooms."

On starting his acting process in Los Angeles

"Glancing back at the years I spent going to America trying out for things and I had, as it were, been jettisoned. I had a large chunk of change to get around. I was going around Los Angeles by transport. It was troublesome. However, look, I surmise we as a whole have our battles."

On battling with a dietary issue

"Truth be told, I think there was a gentle case there. I think some time ago when I was beginning, there was a lot of tension to look a specific way. What's more, they were less discussed by men. Undoubtedly, as a youthful entertainer — susceptible — I was attempting to fit into what was required.

"Send me on this extraordinary excursion; presently I've found out about wellbeing, health, wellness and taught myself in it. What's more, that is the reason I made my foundation wellness stage, My Pinnacle Challenge, which teaches others how to make a sound way of life."

On growing up without knowing his dad

"It's been a truly fascinating excursion and I think the most intriguing part was to know that he's had an impact on my existence without being there. I'm the man today as a result of his nonattendance, I presume. Yet in addition, there are different attributes I think I have that certainly he had too.

"Having said that, you know, I had an astonishing childhood and a superb, extremely caring mother. So I feel extremely lucky."

On what's to come on 'Stranger'

"It's been an unimaginable excursion. We're eight years into recounting the tale of Jamie and Claire, and I surely need to complete the story. However long that goes, I need to realize what occurs toward the end.

"We're right now shooting season seven. It's a major season. We're completing 16 episodes, so we'll see where we get to. Yet, I'm energized by the fans. There's a great deal there."

Printed in Great Britain
by Amazon

17880640R00020